SUMMER MATH WORKBOOK

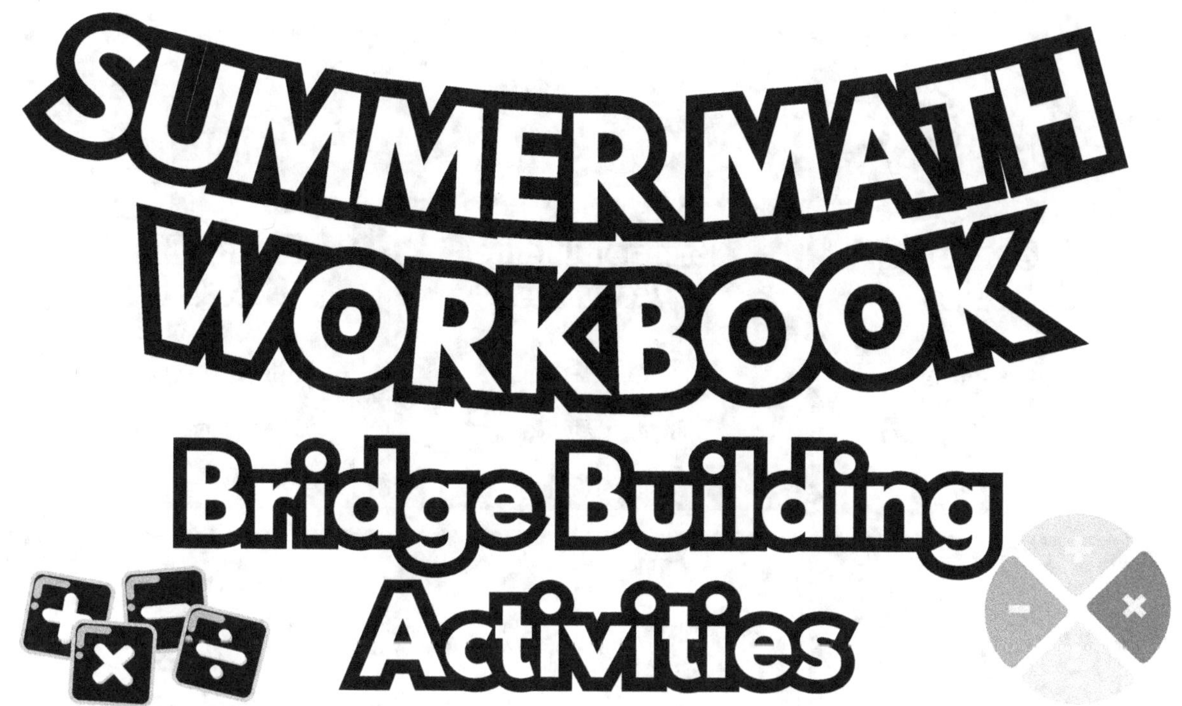

Grade
1 2
SUMMER MATH WORKBOOK
Bridge Building Activities
Number Sense
Addition and Subtraction
Place Value

Grade
2 3
SUMMER MATH WORKBOOK
Bridge Building Activities
Number Sense
Addition and Subtraction
Place Value

Grade
3 4
SUMMER MATH WORKBOOK
Bridge Building Activities
Number Sense
Addition and Subtraction
Place Value

Grade
4 5
SUMMER MATH WORKBOOK
Bridge Building Activities
Multiplication and Division
Place Value and Units
Fractions and Geometry

Grade
5 6
SUMMER MATH WORKBOOK
Bridge Building Activities
Multiplication and Division
Factors and Multiples
Fractions and Geometry

Grade
6 7
SUMMER MATH WORKBOOK
Bridge Building Activities
Arithmetic
Algebra
Geometry and Statistics

Grade
7 8
SUMMER MATH WORKBOOK
Bridge Building Activities
Ratio and Percentage
Algebra and Cartesian Plane
Geometry and Statistics

Grade
8 9
SUMMER MATH WORKBOOK
Bridge Building Activities
Ratio and Percentage
Algebra
Geometry and Graphing

Grade
9 10
SUMMER MATH WORKBOOK
Bridge Building Activities
Factoring and Distributing
Algebra
Geometry and Graphing

Introduction

As parents and educators, we understand the pivotal role that mathematics plays in shaping a child's academic journey and future success. Yet, the path to mathematical proficiency can often seem daunting, filled with challenges and complexities. That's where the transformative power of Summer Bridge Building Activities books comes into play, illuminating the way forward with clarity, precision, and purpose.

Summer vacation is a time for rest and relaxation, but it also presents the risk of the "summer slide," where students lose some of the academic gains they made during the school year. Summer Bridge Building Activities books are specifically designed to tackle this challenge, ensuring that your child stays academically engaged and prepared for the upcoming school year. These books provide a seamless bridge from one grade to the next, reinforcing essential skills and introducing new concepts that will give your child a head start.

Imagine your child eagerly diving into the pages of a Summer Bridge Building Activities book, greeted by clear, engaging content that demystifies complex mathematical concepts. With each turn of the pages, they embark on a journey of discovery, encountering thoughtfully curated practice questions that reinforce learning and sharpen problem-solving skills. As they unveil the answers to those questions, a sense of accomplishment blossoms within them — a tangible reward for their hard work and dedication.

Summer Bridge Building Activities books transcend traditional educational tools; they are meticulously crafted to build a deep and enduring understanding of mathematics. These books follow a sequential and logical progression, starting from fundamental principles and advancing to sophisticated problem-solving strategies. Each chapter is designed to build on the previous one, ensuring a solid and comprehensive foundation for future learning.

Parents, we yearn for nothing more than to see our children thrive academically and personally. We want to witness the spark of inspiration ignited within them as they overcome academic challenges with confidence and poise. Summer Bridge Building Activities books serve as indispensable partners in this noble endeavor, offering not just practice questions but the keys to unlocking a world of academic and personal opportunities.

Visualize the pride on your child's face as they master a challenging math concept, the joy they experience when their efforts yield results, and the confidence they gain with each success. These pages are designed to make learning math a positive, enriching, and deeply rewarding experience that will benefit them throughout their academic journey and beyond.

For educators, Summer Bridge Building Activities books are invaluable allies in the quest to cultivate mathematical proficiency in the classroom. Accompanied by comprehensive guides and readily available answers, instructors can focus on mentoring and nurturing their students, secure in the knowledge that these books provide a robust framework for effective learning.

Within the pages of Summer Bridge Building Activities books lies not just the promise of academic excellence, but the seeds of a brighter future. By integrating these resources into your child's summer routine, you are bestowing upon them the gifts of confidence, curiosity, and a lifelong love of learning.

Invest in your child's future today with Summer Bridge Building Activities books — because every great journey begins with a single step, and this step can change everything. Keep the momentum of learning alive over the summer, and watch your child soar to new academic heights.

Contents

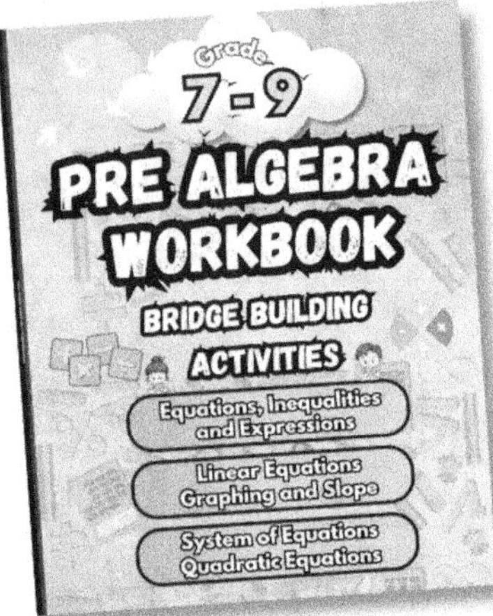

Grade 7 - 9
PRE ALGEBRA WORKBOOK
BRIDGE BUILDING
ACTIVITIES
Equations, Inequalities and Expressions
Linear Equations Graphing and Slope
System of Equations Quadratic Equations

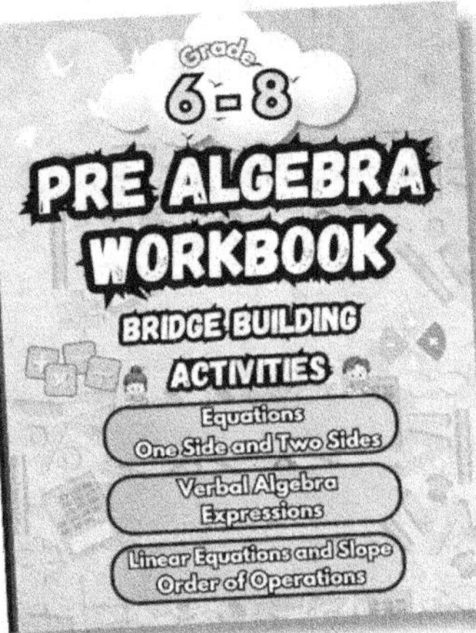

Grade 6 - 8
PRE ALGEBRA WORKBOOK
BRIDGE BUILDING
ACTIVITIES
Equations One Side and Two Sides
Verbal Algebra Expressions
Linear Equations and Slope Order of Operations

Grade 5 - 6
PRE ALGEBRA WORKBOOK
BRIDGE BUILDING
ACTIVITIES
Integers, Mixed Numbers Decimals and Fractions
Place Value Exponents and Roots
Percentage and Ratio Word Problems

PRE ALGEBRA WORKBOOK
for
Beginners
Integers Fractions, Mixed Numbers
Place Value Exponents and Roots
Percentage Ratio Conversion

PRE ALGEBRA WORKBOOK
for
Adults
Integers Percent and Ratio
Equations, Inequalities Expressions
Order of Operations

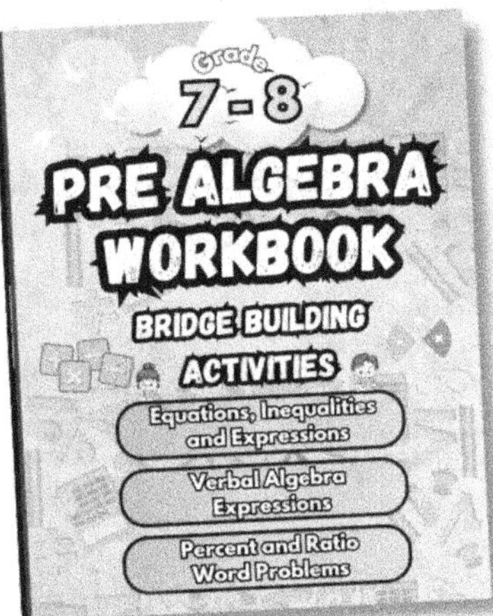

Grade 7 - 8
PRE ALGEBRA WORKBOOK
BRIDGE BUILDING
ACTIVITIES
Equations, Inequalities and Expressions
Verbal Algebra Expressions
Percent and Ratio Word Problems

Grade 9 - 10
PRE ALGEBRA WORKBOOK
BRIDGE BUILDING
ACTIVITIES
Equations and Inequalities Verbal Algebra
Linear and Quadratic Equations
System of Equations Polynomials

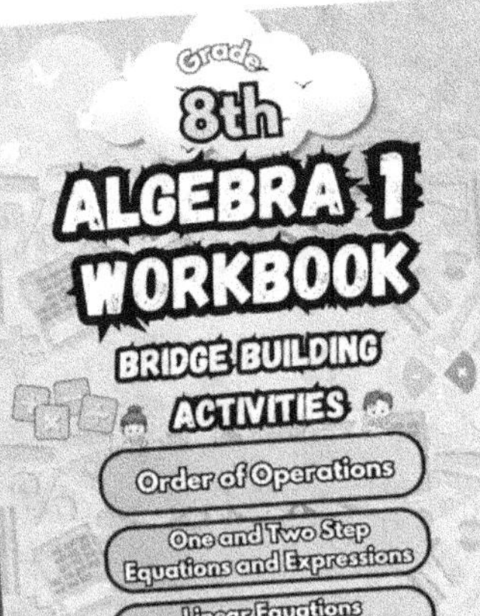

Grade 8th
ALGEBRA 1 WORKBOOK
BRIDGE BUILDING
ACTIVITIES
Order of Operations
One and Two Step Equations and Expressions
Linear Equations Cartesian Plane

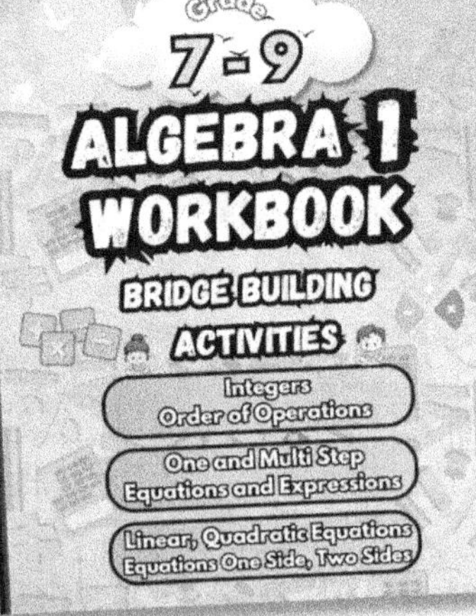

Grade 7 - 9
ALGEBRA 1 WORKBOOK
BRIDGE BUILDING
ACTIVITIES
Integers Order of Operations
One and Multi Step Equations and Expressions
Linear, Quadratic Equations Equations One Side, Two Sides

<u>**Order of Operations (PEMDAS)**</u>

The order of operations, often remembered by the acronym PEMDAS, stands for:

- **Parentheses**: Perform operations inside parentheses first.
- **Exponents**: Evaluate exponents (powers and roots) next.
- **Multiplication and Division**: Perform multiplication and division from left to right.
- **Addition and Subtraction:** Perform addition and subtraction from left to right.

The order of operations helps to clarify which operations should be performed first in a mathematical expression to ensure consistent and accurate results.

- **Parentheses**: Evaluate expressions within parentheses first. If there are nested parentheses, start with the innermost ones and work your way out.

    1. Example: $2 \times (3 + 4) = 2 \times 7 = 14$

- **Exponents**: Evaluate expressions with exponents (powers and roots) next.

    1. Example: $2^3 + 4 = 8 + 4 = 12$

- **Multiplication and Division**: Perform multiplication and division from left to right.

    1. Example: $2 \times 3 + 4 = 6 + 4 = 10$

    2. Example: $6 \div 2 \times 3 = 3 \times 3 = 9$

- **Addition and Subtraction**: Perform addition and subtraction from left to right.

    1. Example: $2 + 3 \times 4 = 2 + 12 = 14$

    2. Example: $10 - 4 \div 2 = 10 - 2 = 8$

Order of Operations (PEMDAS)

Evaluate Expressions.

1. $7 + 6 - 9 + 9 =$

2. $(7^2) \times (8^2) + 3 =$

3. $1 \times (5 + 8) =$

4. $6 + 9 - 7 + 8 =$

5. $7 + 4 + 8 =$

6. $(10 \times 8) - (8 + 2) =$

7. $4 \times 6 =$

8. $3 + 7 - 6 + 1 =$

9. $7 \times (9 + 6) =$

10. $5 \times (1 + 2) =$

11. $(4 + 5) \times (7 + 10) =$

12. $10 \times 2 + 9 =$

13. $6 + 6^2 + 1 + 4^2 =$

14. $(8 \times 5) - (2 + 2) =$

15. $8 \times 1 + 10 =$

16. $1 + 10 + 2 =$

17. $10 \times 3 + 10 =$

18. $7 \times (2 + 2) =$

19. $7 + 6 + 2 =$

20. $10 \times (3 + 6) =$

21. $(7^2) \times (4^2) + 3 =$

22. $10(5 + 9) =$

23. $9 \times (10 + 2) =$

24. $7 + 4 + 2 =$

25. $5 + 2^2 + 4 + 10^2 =$

26. $10 + 8 + 6 =$

27. $(5 + 1)^2 + (1 + 5)^2 =$

28. $3 \times (7 + 4) =$

29. $(8 + 1) \times (2 + 1) =$

30. $5 + 2 - 1 + 3 =$

31. $9 + 9 - 9 + 8 =$

32. $7 + 1^2 =$

33. $3 + 1^2 =$

34. $10 + 4 - 10 + 9 =$

35. $2 + 10^2 + 8 + 8^2 =$

36. $(7 + 4)(4 + 9) =$

37. $5 + 7^2 =$

38. $(9^2) \times (1^2) + 3 =$

39. $(1^2) \times (2^2) + 9 =$

40. $8 + 2 + 2 =$

41. $2 + 1 + 3 =$

42. $4 \times 6 \times 1 =$

43. $(2 + 1) \div 5 =$

44. $3 + 1 - 1 + 2 =$

45. $3 \times 9 =$

46. $3 \times (8 + 4) =$

47. $5 + 4 + 1 =$

48. $8 \times 3 =$

49. $9 + 2 + 10 + 8 =$

50. $6 + 7^2 =$

51. $10(4 + 4) =$

52. $9 \times 2 + 8 =$

53. $(8 + 9) \times (6 + 2) =$

54. $(7 \times 5) - (3 + 10) =$

55. $7 \times 4 =$

56. $7 \times 8 + 8 =$

57. $4 + 9^2 =$

58. $(4 + 5)^2 =$

59. $3 \times 8 =$

60. $1 \times 4 =$

61. $9 \times 5 \times 3 =$

62. $(6 + 3)^2 =$

63. $6 + 5 - 5 + 9 =$

64. $8 + 2 + 10 =$

65. $6 + 2 + 4 + 2 =$

66. $2 + 9 - 9 + 9 =$

67. $9 + 6^2 + 5 + 6^2 =$

68. $(2 \times 1) - (2 + 8) =$

Equations (One Side)

Solve for the variable.

69. $x + 4 = 13$

70. $8 \times y = 56$

71. $81 - 9z = 9$

72. $k \div 9 = 4$

73. $6 - x = 3$

74. $1y - 5 = 5$

75. $9 - m = 2$

76. $8y - 5 = 51$

77. $x + 5 = 6$

78. $4x - 3 = 1$

79. $k - 2 = 2$

80. $2k - 9 = 3$

81. $48 \div y = 6$

82. $4 + y = 5$

83. $10 - x = 4$

84. $4 \times x = 40$

85. $42 \div k = 6$

86. $6k - 3 = 21$

87. $x \times 1 = 4$

88. $k \div 7 = 2$

89. $7m - 2 = 47$

90. $z \times 1 = 6$

91. $2 \times z = 20$

92. $24 \div k = 4$

93. $m \div 8 = 1$

94. $x - 3 = 7$

95. $13 - 5z = 3$

96. $k - 2 = 8$

97. $5k + 3 = 48$

98. $z \times 8 = 80$

99. $2 + 7z = 30$

100. $y \div 4 = 3$

101. $9y + 7 = 34$

102. $k - 5 = 1$

103. $y + 2 = 8$

104. $5 + x = 8$

105. $7 - k = 4$

106. $5 - y = 4$

107. $y \div 10 = 10$

108. $6 - m = 1$

109. $y + 5 = 10$

110. $12 \div m = 6$

111. $10 \times x = 80$

112. $8x + 9 = 25$

113. $k + 2 = 5$

114. $m \times 9 = 90$

115. $10 \div m = 10$

116. $5k - 3 = 27$

117. $2 + 1y = 4$

118. $33 - 3x = 3$

119. $y \div 8 = 9$

120. $y \div 1 = 10$

121. $2m + 10 = 28$

122. $x \div 5 = 4$

123. $7z + 6 = 34$

124. $y \div 1 = 9$

125. $63 \div z = 7$

126. $y - 5 = 5$

127. $9 + z = 14$

128. $9 \times z = 9$

129. $49 \div y = 7$

130. $k + 8 = 12$

131. $6y - 7 = 41$

132. $37 - 9y = 1$

133. $4 \times y = 28$

134. $4x - 8 = 16$

135. $7m + 9 = 72$

136. $3 + y = 11$

137. $k + 4 = 9$

138. $3z + 8 = 32$

<u>**Equations (Two Sides)**</u>

A two-sided equation is an equation where both sides have expressions with variables and constants. The goal when solving a two-sided equation is to find the value of the variable that makes both sides equal.

For example: Let's solve an equation:

$$9 + 8x + 8 = 64 + x + 2$$

- **Combine Like Terms:** Simplify each side of the equation by combining like terms (terms with the same variable or constants).

$$9 + 8x + 8 = 64 + x + 2$$
$$17 + 8x = 66 + x$$

- **Isolate the Variable:** Use inverse operations to isolate the variable on one side of the equation.

subtract x from both sides:

$$17 + 8x - x = 66 + x - x$$

$$17 + 7x = 66$$

subtracting 17 from both sides:

$$17 - 17 + 7x = 66 - 17$$

$$7x = 49$$

divide both sides by 7:

$$\frac{7x}{7} = \frac{49}{7} = x = 7$$

- **Check Solution:** Once you find the solution, substitute it back into the original equation to ensure it makes the equation true.

Substitute $x = 7$ back into the original equation:
$$9 + 8(7) + 8 = 64 + 7 + 2$$
$$9 + 56 + 8 = 64 + 7 + 2$$
$$73 = 73$$

Equations (Two Sides)

Solve for the variable.

139. $2 + 8y = 16 - 6y$

140. $12 + z = 3 + 4z + 3$

141. $23 + z + \text{-}2 = 2 + 4z + 7$

142. $4 + 4k + 6 = 24 - k + 11$

143. $8 + 9z = 72 - 7z$

144. $17 - z = 5 + 5z$

145. $4 + 7z = 58 + z$

146. $13 + k = 7 + 2k + 1$

147. $7x = 40 - x$

148. $24 + k = 7 + 3k + 3$

149. $8x = 42 + x$

150. $8m + 6 = 51 - m$

151. $24 + 2k = 4 + 7k$

152. $6y + 8 = 98 - 4y$

153. $19 - 5z = 7z + 7$

154. $9 + 4k + 8 = 23 + k$

155. $7k = 72 - k$

156. $72 - x = 7x$

157. $7 + 9x = 58 - 8x$

158. $28 - y + 9 = 6 + 8y + 4$

159. $32 - 2x = 6x + 8$

160. $6 + 7x = 78 - x$

161. $38 + k = 5k + 6$

162. $2m = 3 + m$

163. $8m + 1 = 64 - m$

164. $49 - x = 6x + 7$

165. $8x + 16 = 9 + 9x$

166. $26 - x = 8 + 2x$

167. $2 + 5z = 30 + z$

168. $6 + 6z = 76 - 4z$

169. $6 + x = 5 + 2x$

170. $15 + z = 6z$

171. $5 + 7x + 3 = 32 + x$

172. $15 + 8k = 9k + 8$

173. $7m = 40 - m$

174. $8 - k = 7k$

175. $5m = 20 + m$

176. $8 + k = 5k$

177. $149 - 7z = 5 + 9z$

178. $5y + 2 = 3y + 8$

179. $6y = 56 - y$

180. $88 - 6y = 8y + 4$

181. $29 - 2z = 7 + 9z$

182. $10 + 2m = 2 + 4m$

183. $13 + y = 8y + 6$

184. $6y + 7 = 52 + y$

185. $13 + k = 9 + 3k$

186. $42 - y = 4y + 7$

187. $6 + y = 7y$

188. $3 + 2k = 12 + k$

189. $5y = 12 - y$

190. $12 - z = 2z$

191. $20 - 2z = 4 + 6z$

192. $7x = 6 + x$

193. $5 + 7z + 8 = 54 + z + 1$

194. $5k + 8 = 53 - 4k$

195. $2z = 9 + z$

196. $6 + 9x = 42 - 3x$

197. $4 - z = 3z$

198. $23 - m + 9 = 5 + 5m + 3$

199. $48 - x = 3 + 8x$

200. $31 - x + 17 = 7 + 3x + 9$

201. $1 + 5m = 17 + m$

202. $5x + 21 = 9x + 9$

203. $11 + y = 5 + 2y$

204. $3 + x = 2x + 1$

205. $4z + 5 = 23 - 2z$

206. $67 - z = 3 + 7z$

207. $46 - m = 5m + 4$

208. $13 + z = 1 + 3z$

209. $7z + 9 = 2z + 39$

210. $2k = 8 + k$

211. $28 - y = 7 + 2y + 3$

212. $5y + 2 = 38 - y$

213. $8z + 3 = 17 - 6z$

214. $33 + z = 1 + 5z$

215. $56 - y = 6y$

216. $6y = 40 + y$

217. $6 + 7y = 38 - y$

218. $5 + x = 2x$

<u>**Verbal Algebra**</u>

Verbal algebra involves translating word problems or verbal statements into algebraic expressions or equations.

For example: The product of the two numbers is 91. One number is six less than the other. What are the numbers?

We're given a verbal description of a problem, and we need to represent it using algebraic symbols and equations.

Let's break down the given problem into algebraic expressions:

- Given that the product of the two numbers is 91, we can write the equation: $xy = 91$
- Also, given that one number is six less than the other, we can write another equation: $x = y - 6$

Now, we can use algebraic techniques to solve the system of equations to find the values of x and y, which represent the two numbers.

$$x\,(x - 6) = 91$$

1. **Solve the equation:**

   - Expand the equation:

   $$x^2 - 6x = 91$$

   - Rearrange the equation into standard quadratic form:

   $$x^2 - 6x - 91 = 0$$

   - Factor the quadratic equation:

   $$(x - 13)\,(x + 7) = 0$$

2. **Find the solutions for x:**

   - From the factored form, we have two possible values for x:

$$x = 13 \text{ or } x = -7$$

3. **Check the validity of the solutions:**

   - Since one number is six less than the other, we discard the negative solution.

   - Therefore, the solution is $x = 13$.

4. **Find the other number:**

   - Substitute $x = 13$ into the expression for the other number:

   Other number $= x - 6 = 13 - 6 = 7$

So, the two numbers are 13 and 7.

Verbal Algebra Expressions

219. One of two numbers is three-fifths of the other number. The sum of the numbers is 8. Find the numbers.

220. The product of two numbers is 50. One number is five less than the other. What are the numbers?

221. The product of two numbers is 75. One number is ten less than the other. What are the numbers?

222. One-fourth of a number increased by 2 is 3. What is the number?

223. Two more than a number is 5. What is the number?

224. One more than twice a number is equal to the number increased by 10. What is the number?

225. Eight more than four times a number is equal to the number increased by 20. What is the number?

226. A number increased by two is 7. Find the number.

227. Four times a number equals 28 less than eight times the number. What is the number?

228. 30 is equal to the product of five and some number. Find the number.

229. The sum of two consecutive numbers is 15. What are the numbers?

230. Seven more than four times a number is equal to the number increased by 22. What is the number?

231. The product of two numbers is 22. One number is nine less than the other. What are the numbers?

232. Two-fourths of a number diminished by 1 is 1. Find the number.

233. One of two numbers is one-half of the other number. The sum of the numbers is 6. Find the numbers.

234. 10 is equal to the product of two and some number. Find the number.

235. The product of two and a number is 8. What is the number?

236. Four times a number equals 2 less than six times the number. What is the number?

237. One of two numbers is eight more than the other. The sum of the numbers is 10. Find the numbers.

238. Three more than a number is 11. What is the number?

239. Two times a number equals 20 less than six times the number. What is the number?

Evaluate Expressions

Evaluating expressions involves substituting given values for variables in an expression and then performing the indicated operations to find the result.

For example: Let's evaluate $4x - 10$, when $x = 3$:

Step 1: Substitute the given value for the variable:

Replace every occurrence of x in the expression $4x - 10$ with the given value, which is 3:

$$= 4(3) - 10$$

Step 2: Perform the operations:

Perform the indicated operations according to the order of operations (PEMDAS - Parentheses, Exponents, Multiplication and Division, Addition and Subtraction):

$$= 4 \times 3 - 10$$

Step 3: Simplify:

Calculate the result:

$$12 - 10 = 2$$

Evaluate Equations

Evaluate each expression when: x = 2

240. $8 - x =$

241. $2x - 5 + 2x =$

242. $2 + (5x + 3) =$

243. $x(7 + x) =$

244. $2x + 8 + (2x - 4) =$

245. $8 + x =$

246. $2(8x - 3) + 2(5 + x) =$

247. $1(5 - x) =$

248. $2 + x =$

249. $8x + 3 =$

Evaluate Equations

Evaluate each expression when: $x = 5$

250. $1(10x) =$

251. $3x + 6 =$

252. $9 + x =$

253. $4x + 5 =$

254. $1 + 5x =$

255. $9x + 4 =$

256. $3x + 9 =$

257. $7x - 4 + 3x =$

258. $9 + \dfrac{x}{5} =$

259. $6 + 3x =$

Evaluate Equations

Evaluate each expression when: $x = 5$

260. $10x - 5 =$

261. $2(1 + x) =$

262. $2(8x - 10) + 6(6 + x) =$

263. $7(10x) =$

264. $(x)(4x) =$

265. $5x - x =$

266. $6x + 7 =$

267. $8x + 7 =$

268. $(2x + 9) + (8x - 3) =$

269. $(x^1 + 4) - 5(7 + x) =$

Evaluate Equations

Evaluate each expression when: $x = 7$

270. $x + 9x + 6x =$

271. $x + 6 + 4x =$

272. $7 \div (x + 6) =$

273. $10(10 + x) =$

274. $8x + 2 =$

275. $8x + 10 =$

276. $2 + (8x + 4) =$

277. $5x + 6 + (9x - 10) =$

278. $(3x)(10x) =$

279. $x(4 + x) =$

SUMMER ALGEBRA WORKBOOK

Evaluate Equations

Evaluate each expression when: $x = 4$

280. $4x + 5x + 2x =$

281. $8x + x =$

282. $7(x - 9) + 2(1 + x) =$

283. $6x - 2 + 9x =$

284. $5x + 5x - 10 =$

285. $3 + \dfrac{x}{2} =$

286. $5(6 - x) =$

287. $7x + x =$

288. $6(2 + x) =$

289. $x(4 + x) =$

Evaluate Equations

Evaluate each expression when: $x = 4$

290. $5(8 - x) =$

291. $3x + 2 =$

292. $7 + (9x + 9) =$

293. $x \div 2 =$

294. $x + 9 - 8x =$

295. $5x + 6x + 8x =$

296. $3 + 6x =$

297. $7x + 3 =$

298. $10x + 4 - 8x =$

299. $x^1 + x - 4 =$

Evaluate Equations

Evaluate each expression when: $x = 2$

300. $9x + 3 =$

301. $5x + 1 + (2x - 5) =$

302. $3 + x =$

303. $x - 9 =$

304. $7x - 3 + 9x =$

305. $x + 7 =$

306. $6x + x =$

307. $6x + 7 =$

308. $(x + 8) \div 1 =$

309. $8 \div x + 1 =$

Solving Inequalities

Inequalities are mathematical expressions that compare the relative sizes of two values. They are used to express relationships where one quantity is:

- "<" (less than),
- ">" (greater than),
- "<=" (less than or equal to),
- ">=" (greater than or equal to),
- and "≠" (not equal to) another quantity.

For example:

$$y + \text{-}10 \leq \text{-}8$$

To isolate y, we need to get rid of the constant term -10. Since -10 is being subtracted from y, we can undo this operation by adding 10 to both sides of the inequality:

$$y - 10 + 10 \leq -8 + 10$$

$$y \leq 2$$

To check the solution:

$$2 - 10 \leq -8$$

$$-8 = -8$$

The inequality is true when $y = 2$

Solving Inequalities

310.

$$k - {-4} \leq 3$$

311.

$$8x > 6$$

312.

$$-2 + x \geq 2$$

313.

$$\frac{m}{2} > 7$$

314.

$$m + 2 \leq -3$$

315.

$$-9 - x \leq 0$$

316.

$$\frac{x}{-8} \leq -6$$

317.

$$-21z \geq 12$$

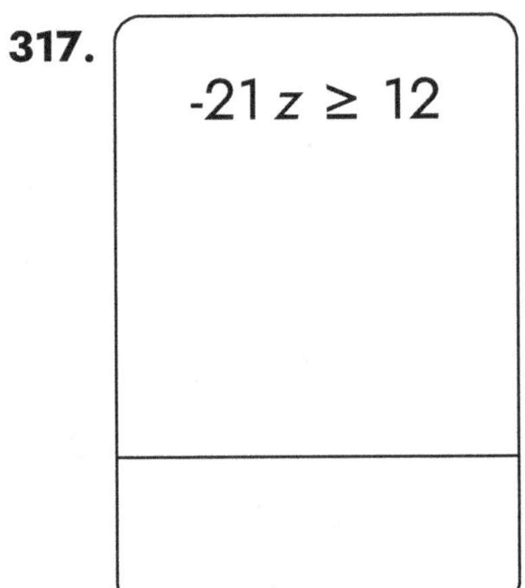

318.

$$-6 \leq \frac{x}{-3}$$

319.

$$18z \geq 15$$

320.

$$x - 2 \leq 9$$

321.

$$9 > y + -2$$

322.

$$y + 2 \geq -3$$

323.

$$-6 \leq \frac{z}{2}$$

324.

$$-1 < -3 - y$$

325.

$$12\,k < -8$$

326.

$$-3 + k \geq 2$$

327.

$$4 > \frac{y}{5}$$

328.

$$8\,k < 4$$

329.

$$k - 6 \geq 9$$

330.

$$y - 5 \leq 6$$

331.

$$-18\,y \leq 12$$

332.

$$5 > 7 + z$$

333.

$$-4 \geq \frac{z}{7}$$

334.

$$12 > -18x$$

335.

$$-6 - x \geq -1$$

336.

$$-2 > -6 + y$$

337.

$$-8 < \frac{z}{8}$$

338.

$$4x \le -5$$

339.

$$x + -5 < 8$$

340.

$$-2 < \frac{x}{4}$$

341.

$$-3 - k > 9$$

342.

$$-6 > -1 + y$$

343.

$$10 > 8z$$

344.

$$-2 > \dfrac{k}{-6}$$

345.

$$9 \leq x - -5$$

346.

$$-6z \geq -12$$

347.

$$-6 < \frac{x}{5}$$

348.

$$k - 5 < 7$$

349.

$$-8 + m \leq 9$$

<u>**Ratio and Proportion Word Problems**</u>

We can use the concept of proportionality in solving many word problems, for example:

If a car travels 620 miles in six hours, how far can it travel in 12 hours?

Since the car travels a certain distance in a certain amount of time, we can assume that the distance traveled is directly proportional to the time taken.

Let d be the distance the car can travel in 12 hours.

We can set up a proportion:

$$\frac{\text{Distance1}}{\text{Time1}} = \frac{\text{Distance2}}{\text{Time2}}$$

Substituting the given values:

$$\frac{620 \text{ miles}}{6 \text{ hours}} = \frac{d}{12 \text{ hours}}$$

Now, let's solve for d:

$$d = \frac{620 \times 12}{6} = \frac{7440}{6} = 1240$$

So, the car can travel 1240 miles in 12 hours.

Ratio and Proportion Word Problems

350. If it takes eight students 17 hours to complete a science project, how many students are needed to finish the project in nine hours?

351. If a recipe calls for six eggs for every six cups of flour, how many eggs are needed for 16 cups of flour?

352. A bike travels at a speed of 24 miles per hour. How long will it take to travel 90 miles?

353. If a square has an area of 139 square meters, what is the length of each side of the square?

354. If a recipe calls for three eggs for every six cups of flour, how many eggs are needed for eight cups of flour?

355. A charity received a donation of $2,917 from a company. If the donation was divided among five charities in the ratio 2:3:4:5:6, how much did the fifth charity receive?

356. A machine can produce 184 units of a product in eight hours. How long will it take to produce 343 units?

357. Emmett drives 118 miles in five hours. How far can he travel in 11 hours?

358. If a recipe calls for five cups of sugar for every eight cups of flour, how many cups of sugar are needed for 12 cups of flour?

359. If a car travels 585 miles in six hours, how far can it travel in 10 hours?

360. If three workers can build a wall in 20 hours, how many workers are needed to build the wall in eight hours?

361. A train travels 256 miles in three hours. How far can it travel in 15 hours?

362. If six workers can complete a job in 19 days, how many workers are needed to complete the job in six days?

363. A charity received a donation of $1,909 from a company. If the donation was divided among five charities in the ratio 2:3:4:5:6, how much did the third charity receive?

364. A bus travels at a speed of 87 miles per hour. How long will it take to travel 146 miles?

365. If a map scale is 1 inch to seven miles, how far apart are two cities that are three inches apart on the map?

366. Audrey sells five folders for every eight purses. If there are 97 folders, how many purses are there?

367. A train travels 127 miles in four hours. How far can it travel in seven hours?

368. In a bag of candies, the ratio of chocolate candies to fruit candies is five:six. If there are 16 fruit candies, how many chocolate candies are there?

369. If 10 workers can build a house in 20 hours, how many workers are needed to build the house in five hours?

370. A car travels 288 miles in three hours. How far can it travel in six hours?

Percent Word Problems

371. Ellie bought a book for $25.00. If she paid an additional 12% for sales tax, how much in total did she pay for the book?

372. A store offers a 5% discount on all items. If Audrey buys globes originally priced at $40.00, how much money did she save?

373. In a class of 60 students, 5% are girls. How many are girls?

374. A restaurant makes a pizza that is 20 inches in diameter. If they want to increase the size of the pizza by 5%, what will be the new diameter?

375. Nova bought some tissues for $100.00. If she paid an additional 55% for sales tax, how much in total did she pay for the tissues?

376. In a school of 40 students, 5% of them take the bus to school. How many students take the bus?

377. In a class of 20 students, 30% are boys. How many are boys?

378. Benjamin buys headphones for $60.00 to sell them in market. If he wants to earn 30% profit. What must be the selling price of headphones?

379. A school has a total of 60 teachers. If 5% of them are men, how many female teachers are there?

380. A car dealership sold 80 cars last month. If the sales increased by 55% this month, how many cars did they sell this month?

381. In a basket of 40 shoes, 5% are red shoes . How many are red shoes?

382. Tristan had 60 gloves. He gave away 5% of them. How many did he have left?

383. If the number 60 is decreased by 5%, what is the value of the new number?

384. In a survey of 90 people, 30% said they preferred android OS. How many people preferred android OS?

385. Gemma bought pencils for $80.00. If she paid an additional 5% for sales tax, how much in total did she pay for the pencils?

386. A school has 80 students. If 5% of them play baseball, how many students play baseball?

387. In a survey of 40 people, 55% said they prefer cats over dogs. How many people prefer cats?

388. Elijah's monthly sales of scalpels was $80.00. If he earned 5% of profit, what was his profit?

389. Bella bought a pizza for $75.00. If she paid an additional 12% for sales tax, how much in total did she pay for the pizza?

390. A teacher gave a math test with 50 questions. If a student got 12% questions correct, how many questions were correct?

ANSWERS

Page 1: Order of Operations (PEMDAS)

1. 13	**2.** 3,139	**3.** 13	**4.** 16	**5.** 19	**6.** 70	**7.** 24	**8.** 5
9. 105	**10.** 15	**11.** 153	**12.** 29	**13.** 59	**14.** 36	**15.** 18	**16.** 13
17. 40	**18.** 28	**19.** 15	**20.** 90	**21.** 787	**22.** 140	**23.** 108	**24.** 13
25. 113	**26.** 24	**27.** 72	**28.** 33	**29.** 27	**30.** 9	**31.** 17	**32.** 8
33. 4	**34.** 13	**35.** 174	**36.** 143	**37.** 54	**38.** 84	**39.** 13	**40.** 12
41. 6	**42.** 24	**43.** 0.6	**44.** 5	**45.** 27	**46.** 36	**47.** 10	**48.** 24
49. 29	**50.** 55	**51.** 80	**52.** 26	**53.** 136	**54.** 22	**55.** 28	**56.** 64
57. 85	**58.** 81	**59.** 24	**60.** 4	**61.** 135	**62.** 81	**63.** 15	**64.** 20
65. 14	**66.** 11	**67.** 86	**68.** -8				

Page 8: Equations (One Side)

69. $x = 9$	**70.** $y = 7$	**71.** $z = 8$	**72.** $k = 36$	**73.** $x = 3$
74. $y = 10$	**75.** $m = 7$	**76.** $y = 7$	**77.** $x = 1$	**78.** $x = 1$
79. $k = 4$	**80.** $k = 6$	**81.** $y = 8$	**82.** $y = 1$	**83.** $x = 6$
84. $x = 10$	**85.** $k = 7$	**86.** $k = 4$	**87.** $x = 4$	**88.** $k = 14$
89. $m = 7$	**90.** $z = 6$	**91.** $z = 10$	**92.** $k = 6$	**93.** $m = 8$
94. $x = 10$	**95.** $z = 2$	**96.** $k = 10$	**97.** $k = 9$	**98.** $z = 10$
99. $z = 4$	**100.** $y = 12$	**101.** $y = 3$	**102.** $k = 6$	**103.** $y = 6$
104. $x = 3$	**105.** $k = 3$	**106.** $y = 1$	**107.** $y = 100$	**108.** $m = 5$
109. $y = 5$	**110.** $m = 2$	**111.** $x = 8$	**112.** $x = 2$	**113.** $k = 3$

114. m = 10   **115.** m = 1   **116.** k = 6   **117.** y = 2   **118.** x = 10

119. y = 72   **120.** y = 10   **121.** m = 9   **122.** x = 20   **123.** z = 4

124. y = 9   **125.** z = 9   **126.** y = 10   **127.** z = 5   **128.** z = 1

129. y = 7   **130.** k = 4   **131.** y = 8   **132.** y = 4   **133.** y = 7

134. x = 6   **135.** m = 9   **136.** y = 8   **137.** k = 5   **138.** z = 8

Page 15: Equations (Two Sides)

139. y = 1   **140.** z = 2   **141.** z = 4   **142.** k = 5   **143.** z = 4   **144.** z = 2

145. z = 9   **146.** k = 5   **147.** x = 5   **148.** k = 7   **149.** x = 6   **150.** m = 5

151. k = 4   **152.** y = 9   **153.** z = 1   **154.** k − 2   **155.** k = 9   **156.** x = 9

157. x = 3   **158.** y = 3   **159.** x = 3   **160.** x = 9   **161.** k = 8   **162.** m = 3

163. m = 7   **164.** x = 6   **165.** x = 7   **166.** x = 6   **167.** z = 7   **168.** z = 7

169. x = 1   **170.** z = 3   **171.** x = 4   **172.** k = 7   **173.** m = 5   **174.** k = 1

175. m = 5   **176.** k = 2   **177.** z = 9   **178.** y = 3   **179.** y = 8   **180.** y = 6

181. z = 2   **182.** m = 4   **183.** y = 1   **184.** y = 9   **185.** k = 2   **186.** y = 7

187. y = 1   **188.** k = 9   **189.** y = 2   **190.** z = 4   **191.** z = 2   **192.** x = 1

193. z = 7   **194.** k = 5   **195.** z = 9   **196.** x = 3   **197.** z = 1   **198.** m = 4

199. x = 5   **200.** x = 8   **201.** m = 4   **202.** x = 3   **203.** y = 6   **204.** x = 2

205. z = 3   **206.** z = 8   **207.** m = 7   **208.** z = 6   **209.** z = 6   **210.** k = 8

211. y = 6   **212.** y = 6   **213.** z = 1   **214.** z = 8   **215.** y = 8   **216.** y = 8

217. y = 4   **218.** x = 5

Page 23: Verbal Algebra Expressions

219. 5, 3   **220.** 10, 5   **221.** 15, 5   **222.** 4   **223.** 3   **224.** 9

225. 4   **226.** 5   **227.** 7   **228.** 6   **229.** 7, 8   **230.** 5

231. 11, 2   **232.** 4   **233.** 4, 2   **234.** 5   **235.** 4   **236.** 1

237. 1, 9   **238.** 8   **239.** 5

Page 28: Evaluate Equations

240. 6   **241.** 3   **242.** 15   **243.** 18   **244.** 12   **245.** 10   **246.** 40   **247.** 3

248. 4   **249.** 19

Page 29: Evaluate Equations

250. 50   **251.** 21   **252.** 14   **253.** 25   **254.** 26   **255.** 49   **256.** 24   **257.** 46

258. 10   **259.** 21

Page 30: Evaluate Equations

260. 45   **261.** 12   **262.** 126   **263.** 350   **264.** 100   **265.** 20   **266.** 37

267. 47   **268.** 56   **269.** -51

Page 31: Evaluate Equations

270. 112   **271.** 41   **272.** 0.5   **273.** 170   **274.** 58   **275.** 66

276. 62   **277.** 94   **278.** 1,470   **279.** 77

Page 32: Evaluate Equations

280. 44   **281.** 36   **282.** -25   **283.** 58   **284.** 30   **285.** 5   **286.** 10   **287.** 32

288. 36   **289.** 32

Page 33: Evaluate Equations

290. 20   **291.** 14   **292.** 52   **293.** 2   **294.** -19   **295.** 76   **296.** 27   **297.** 31

298. 12   **299.** 4

Page 34: Evaluate Equations

300. 21   **301.** 10   **302.** 5   **303.** -7   **304.** 29   **305.** 9   **306.** 14   **307.** 19

308. 10   **309.** 5

Page 35:   Solving Inequalities

310. k ≤ -1   **311.** x > 3/4   **312.** x ≥ 4   **313.** m > 14   **314.** m ≤ -5

315. x ≥ -9   **316.** x ≥ 48   **317.** z ≤ -4/7   **318.** x ≤ 18   **319.** z ≥ 5/6

320. x ≤ 11   **321.** y < 11   **322.** y ≥ -5   **323.** z ≥ -12   **324.** y < -2

325. k < -2/3   **326.** k ≥ 5   **327.** y < 20   **328.** k < 1/2   **329.** k ≥ 15

330. y ≤ 11   **331.** y ≥ -2/3   **332.** z < -2   **333.** z ≤ -28   **334.** x > -2/3

335. x ≤ -5   **336.** y < 4   **337.** z > -64   **338.** x ≤ -5/4   **339.** x < 13

340. x > -8   **341.** k < -12   **342.** y < -5   **343.** z < 5/4   **344.** k > 12

345. x ≥ 4   **346.** z ≤ 2   **347.** x > -30   **348.** k < 12   **349.** m ≤ 17

Page 45:   Ratio and Proportion Word Problems

350. 15.11   **351.** 16   **352.** 3.75   **353.** 11.79   **354.** 4

355. 875.1   **356.** 14.91   **357.** 259.6   **358.** 7.5   **359.** 975

360. 7.5   **361.** 1,280   **362.** 19   **363.** 381.8   **364.** 1.68

365. 21   **366.** 155.2   **367.** 222.25   **368.** 13.33   **369.** 40

370. 576

Page 52:   Percent Word Problems

371. $28.00   **372.** $2.00   **373.** 3   **374.** 21   **375.** $155.00

376. 2   **377.** 6   **378.** $78.00   **379.** 57   **380.** 124

381. 2   **382.** 57   **383.** 57   **384.** 27   **385.** $84.00

386. 4   **387.** 22   **388.** $4.00   **389.** $84.00   **390.** 6